Snap books® Girl Talk

Lunch Lines, Tryouts, and Making the Grade

Questions and Answers About School

by Nancy Loewen and Paula Skelley
illustrated by Julissa Mora

Content adviser:
John E. Desrochers, PhD

CAPSTONE PRESS
a capstone imprint

Table of Contents

What's one thing that nearly all kids have in common?

School!

School is a pretty amazing place. It's where you go to class, play sports and music, and hang with friends.

BUT SCHOOL CAN SEEM LIKE AN OBSTACLE COURSE.

Every day you need to make a ton of decisions. Who should you sit with at lunch? Should you speak up or keep quiet? Will you study hard or do just enough to pass?

It never hurts to get good advice, especially about school. We know exactly what you're going through. We've been there! If you find our suggestions helpful—great! And if there are some things you can't quite work through on your own, talk to a trusted adult. Parents, teachers, and school counselors are ready to help.

In the Classroom

Q I feel like everybody stares at me when I ask a question in class. But if I don't ask questions, I get bad grades, and then I feel even worse! What can I do?

A Lots of kids are scared to ask questions in front of the class. They're afraid it makes them look dumb. But asking questions is actually a smart thing to do because that's how you learn! Besides, other kids might be wondering the same thing you are.

You can always talk to your teacher when other kids aren't around. Pick a time before or after school. If there's no time to talk, e-mail your teacher. Teachers expect questions and are willing to help out.

Q I'm not very good at reading out loud. How can I get better at it so the other kids won't make fun of me?

A You probably know the answer already: Practice. Read to your parents, grandparents, brothers, and sisters. Don't worry about reading fast right away. Take your time. If you come to a word you don't know, sound it out, syllable by syllable. Repeat it a few times, and keep on reading.

Go to the library and check out a book and the audio book with the same title. Then you can read out loud along with the audio. This is a good way to hear how words are supposed to be pronounced.

If it seems like letters are getting turned around, or you have trouble seeing clearly, tell your parents or teacher. They'll get you the help you need.

Q I get really nervous when I take tests. No matter how hard I study, I forget half of it as soon as the test is handed out. How can I calm down and do my best?

A Get a good night's sleep the night before. It's tough to do well on a test if you're tired. And don't skip breakfast! Low-sugar cereal, yogurt, and fruit should hit the spot.

Right before your test, take slow, deep breaths. When you breathe deeply, your brain gets more oxygen, which makes it easier to think. Once you feel calmer, tell yourself, "I have studied, and I know the answers."

Tip Clip

Don't be afraid to ask your teacher questions. It's better to know something for sure than to guess. Besides, it's your teacher's job to make sure you are learning.

Q My teacher has us do a lot of group projects. But some kids don't do their share. How can we work together in a way that's fair for everyone?

A Start with a plan. As soon as you get the assignment, make a list of everything that needs to get done. Then divide the work evenly. Make sure everyone knows what he or she is supposed to do. Without a plan, some kids aren't sure what to do next, so they don't do anything.

If certain kids aren't doing their part, remind them what they're supposed to do. If they don't listen, ask your teacher for help.

Q I feel terrible when I get anything less than an A. My teacher and parents keep saying I shouldn't worry so much about my grades. But I can't help it!

A It's great that you want to do the best job you can. But no one is perfect, and no one expects you to be perfect. It's the effort that counts. Really! So just do your best, and don't stress out. A few months from now, will you even remember a certain test or assignment? Probably not!

Q Twice a week, I get pulled out of my regular class to go to a gifted and talented class. Some kids think I'm showing off, but I'm not! Should I tell my parents I don't want to go to the classes anymore?

A Stay in the classes. You'll learn more and get to be around other kids who share the same interests. Don't brag or do anything to draw attention to yourself when you leave class or when you come back. Make a point of treating everyone the way you'd want to be treated. If kids who are giving you a hard time see that you're not looking down on them, they should lighten up.

Q I don't always do so well on homework or tests. I keep making such dumb mistakes!

A A lot of time, just slowing down will help. Don't rush through your homework. Double-check your worksheets or tests before handing them in. Did you answer all the questions? Are your answers complete? Is your writing readable? If you're still making lots of mistakes, talk to your teacher. He or she may have some ideas on how to improve your work in class.

Tip Clip

Grades are important, but they're not the whole story. Try your best, and you'll learn a lot. That's the most important thing.

Teachers

Q My classmates and I really like our teacher. How can we show her how cool we think she is?

A By showing her how cool YOU are. When you and your classmates behave well, she'll know that her students respect her. So get your homework done on time, and listen in class. That will make her feel great!

Q My teacher is going to have a baby soon, and a different teacher will be taking her place. What if I don't like the new teacher?

A Change can be scary. Give the new teacher a chance. Who knows? Maybe you'll really like him or her. Even if you don't, remember that it's for only part of the school year. Focus on the things you can control, like listening, doing your work, and trying your best. If you do those things, everything else will go more smoothly.

Q Some kids are mean to our substitute teachers. And some substitute teachers are tough. Is there anything my friends and I can do to make things go better?

A Teachers are supposed to be in charge of their classrooms. That's their job, right? So when kids act up, teachers might SEEM tough, when really they are just trying to keep things under control. Set a good example for the rest of the class by showing respect and following instructions. If your classmates do things they shouldn't, ask them to stop.

Q Sometimes I don't think my teacher is being fair to me. Should I talk to her or let my mom and dad take care of it?

A It's better to talk to the teacher yourself to see if you can work things out. Give her examples of times you think she was unfair. Your teacher will understand you better—and you will understand her better too. You'll feel proud of yourself because you solved your own problem.

If you don't feel comfortable talking directly to your teacher, ask your parents to get involved.

Tip Clip

Teachers are people too. They make mistakes. And sometimes your personalities just won't click. But if you're respectful no matter what, you'll get along better in the classroom.

Q There's a new student in our class who is autistic. How are we supposed to act around him?

A With respect and kindness, no matter what his differences are. Then just follow his lead. Some kids with autism take a long time to warm up to others. Don't take it personally or try to force a friendship. Once you know him, you won't have to think twice about how to act.

Q A few girls are always saying mean things to me. How can I get them to leave me alone? And how can I keep the other kids from believing the awful things these girls say about me?

A Be strong. You know the truth and so do your friends. But you need to explain things to your teacher and parents. Those girls are bullying you, and that's totally against the rules.

Tell your good friends what's going on, and ask them to stick up for you with the other kids. But try not to worry too much. Your classmates likely know what's really going on.

Q One of my classmates wears a head scarf to school every day. I think it's really pretty, and I want to tell her. But my friends say I shouldn't, that it would be embarrassing. What do you think?

A Tell her. Wouldn't you want someone to tell YOU you looked nice? Besides, it might open the door for a longer talk. You can learn more about her background and why she wears a scarf. It's fun to learn about the things that make us different from one another.

Tip Clip

Don't just stick to your usual friend group. Get to know as many of your classmates as you can. You never know when a new friendship might start up.

Q The boys who sit next to me are always goofing off. It's hard for me to pay attention to the teacher. How can I get them to stop?

A First try asking them, in a nice way, to be quiet. If that doesn't work, talk to your teacher. There's a lot happening in a classroom, and teachers might miss things. Describe the problem and how it's affecting you. Once your teacher knows what's going on, he or she can help. Most teachers won't let on who told.

Q Sometimes the older kids at my school pick on the younger kids. Why do they act that way, and what can we do about it?

A Some kids tease because they don't feel good about themselves. When they make others feel bad, they feel more important. Some kids tease just because it's a habit—a bad habit. They don't even think about what they're doing.

Whatever the reason, you should stick up for the younger kids. If you had a little brother or sister, would you want someone treating him or her that way? Bullying isn't cool, especially bullying someone who is smaller and weaker than you. Tell a trusted adult so no one gets hurt.

Tip Clip

Being by yourself sometimes doesn't mean there's anything wrong with you. Learn to feel comfortable standing apart. Your confidence may even gain you some friendships!

Fitting In

Q I just got "dumped" by my group, and now I don't have anyone to hang out with. What can I do?

A Cliques are tough to deal with. It's hard to lose friends and feel left out. Look around—are other kids dealing with the same thing? Get to know them better, and then you won't feel so alone. Follow your interests. Get involved in group activities, like sports, choir, or theater. Get to know people one-on-one, and pretty soon it won't matter if you're in a clique or not. You'll have friends wherever you go.

Q My mom and I moved to a new city in the middle of the school year. I've never been "the new kid" before. I wish I could wave a magic wand and fit in with my new classmates.

A Being the new kid can be hard, for sure! Be yourself, and look for kids who are friendly or who like the same things you do. Join after-school activities or clubs. It might take a little while, but you will make new friends. Meanwhile, smile, and remember that you had friends before and you will have friends again.

Q A lot of kids at school don't talk to me because I'm in a wheelchair. It's like I'm invisible. How do I let them know that I'm just like them, except I can't walk?

A You may be the first kid they know who uses a wheelchair. They might be worried about saying the wrong thing, so they don't say anything at all. Make an extra effort to talk to kids while you're doing everyday school things. If you're comfortable enough, share with them why you're in a wheelchair. Be open to questions. They'll start to see that you're just like them.

Some schools have programs that teach kids about what it's like to have a physical disability. They even let kids try wheelchairs for themselves. Could you or your parents talk to your principal about doing a program like that at your school? You'd all learn a lot and have fun too.

Q My friends all have something they're really good at in school. I'm never the best at anything. What's wrong with me?

A Nothing is wrong with you. Just because you haven't found your special talent yet doesn't mean you don't have one! Keep trying different things. And don't worry about whether you're the "best" or not. Do things because you enjoy them, try hard, and be proud of yourself.

Q In gym class, I'm always the last one picked for a team. I should be used to it by now, but it still hurts.

A It never feels good to get picked last. Talk to your gym teacher. Instead of picking teams, maybe kids could number off. Or maybe teams could be picked alphabetically. Both of these ways would save some hurt feelings.

Gym might be more fun for you if you work on your skills outside of class. Play team sports with your family or friends just for fun. Usually, the more you practice, the better you'll get.

Remember that not everyone is good at everything. Pay attention to the things you do well. Are you a good artist? Do you get good grades? Do you play an instrument or sing? Those things matter just as much as gym class.

Q My mom drives me to school every morning and waits until I go into the building before she leaves. Sometimes she waves. It's embarrassing. I'm not a little kid!

A You're not a little kid, but you're HER kid, and she loves you. She probably can't help herself. See if she will compromise by parking a little farther away. Ask her not to wave. Instead, say goodbye in the car. That way both of you can start your day on a good note.

Q I like school, and I get good grades, but my friends think that's all I am—smart. I don't want to be called "Professor" or "Brainiac" all the time. I want to be cool! Is it possible to be both?

A Yes! You might have trouble believing it right now, but being smart IS cool. Be proud of your good grades! And of course you're more than your report card. What activities are you in? What kinds of things really interest you? Talk about those things with your friends. Be sure to ask your friends questions about their lives too.

If you're really hurt by the teasing, be honest. Tell them you don't like it. But remember, just because they call you "Professor" doesn't mean they don't think you're cool.

Tip Clip

If you notice someone who's alone, make a point of reaching out. You'll both feel great!

School Activities and Homework

Q This year my school doesn't have enough money to let us take our yearly field trip to the zoo. My friends and I would like to help. What can we do?

A Talk to your principal, teachers, and parents, and let them know how important this field trip is to you. Brainstorm until you find a fund-raiser that's OK with your school. There are lots of ways to raise money. You could hold a bake sale, a car wash, or a silent auction. The businesses in your neighborhood may want to help too. You'll need to find one or two adults who are willing to be in charge. Once you've figured out a plan, you and your friends can spread the word and get lots of families to pitch in. Good luck!

Q On days when I have a lot of activities, I have to stay up late to get my homework done. Then I'm tired the next day at school. What should I do?

A Activities are great, but nothing should come before your schoolwork. And being tired all the time is no fun. The easiest thing would be to take a good look at your activities. Which are the most important to you? Could you cut back on any? Give some up completely? Talk to your parents and see if you can work something out.

It'll be tougher if you don't want to give anything up. You'll need to start planning better. Make the most of the time you're given in class to get your work done. If you have big assignments that will take more than a day, break them down into chunks. Figure out which chunks you can do on which days. Try to do your difficult subjects first, when you've got the most energy. Can you do homework on the bus? In the car? Sometimes you might have to use some of your weekend time to catch up.

Q Every time I sit down to do my homework, I get distracted. How can I stay focused?

A Here are some tips to try:

Figure out the best time of day to do your homework. Do you like to get it all done as soon as you get home from school? Or do you need a break first? Are you more focused right before supper or after? Do you work better sitting down for a big chunk of time or for shorter times, with breaks in between? Once you figure out a time, stick to it every day. You'll train your brain to get used to the new homework schedule.

Get rid of the distractions you have control over. Turn off all the electronics (that includes the TV). Put away the new book you're reading or notes from friends. Clear your work space of clutter. Make sure you're not too hot or too cold.

Pick a spot away from the busiest parts of the house. Instead of working at the kitchen table, find a quiet spot someplace else. If you have a desk in your room, you could work there—unless being in your room is distracting. Ask your parents if you could work in their bedroom or office, or in a guest room.

Get all the supplies you'll need for your homework before you sit down. That way you won't have to keep getting up and looking for things.

Ask a parent or an older brother or sister to sit with you and read or do something quiet while you're doing your homework. Sometimes just being around other people who are focused can help you stay on track.

Do you know someone who is really good at getting homework done on time? Ask him or her for advice.

Q I tried out for a lead role in the school play, but I didn't get it. Instead, I'm one of the "extras." I don't think I want to be in the play at all now. If I'm not the lead, why bother?

A Being an extra will give you some good experience. It also means you'll have a better chance of getting a lead the next time you try out. Plus, being in a play is a lot of fun! It takes all sorts of creative people to put on a good play, not just actors. Someone has to build the set, manage the props, do the lighting and sound, and round up the costumes. And extras are more important than you think. What would a play be like with a mostly empty stage? Do your best, learn all you can, and keep trying for that lead role.

Q I want to be in the science fair this year. But it's the same day as my best friend's birthday party. How do I decide which one to go to?

A Did you say yes to one event before you found out about the other? If you did, you should stick with the first one. If not, you'll need to think it through. What's most important to you? Do you want to be at your friend's party or can you celebrate on another day? Can you work on science projects on your own or do you want take part in the competition? Whatever you decide, remember that there will be more science fairs and more birthday parties to come.

Q Everything's a competition in my school. But what if I don't like to compete?

A Some people like to compete because it makes them try harder. It makes them feel like they've achieved something. Other people don't do as well under pressure. But you should be able to find things to do that aren't based on winning or losing. How about band, choir, or theater? Take an after-school art class, join a book club, or volunteer at a local animal shelter. If you don't want to compete, don't. Be yourself.

Tip Clip

Don't do the same activities all the time. Try something new. You'll get to know a different group of people, and you might discover a talent you never knew you had.

Lunchtime

Q Our lunchroom is so huge, sometimes I can't find my friends! Is it OK to sit by myself or with people I don't know?

A It's fun to sit by your friends at lunch. But whether your lunchroom is big or small, that's not always possible. So if you can't sit by your friends, sit anywhere you want. Talk to the kids next to you. Maybe you'll make new friends. If you'd rather sit by yourself, that's OK too. Be friendly, no matter where you end up. You might feel like everyone is looking at you. But don't worry. They're probably too busy eating and talking to notice who you're sitting with.

Q I have a bad peanut allergy. Some kids in school think it's funny to tease me about it. How do I tell them my allergy isn't a joke?

A Food allergies are serious. People can get really sick or even die from them. You should tell your lunchroom monitor or teacher about the teasing. Most school lunchrooms have rules about teasing and food allergies. Tell your parents too. Maybe the adults can come up with a plan to educate the whole school on how to handle food allergies.

Q My dad likes to draw cartoons on my lunch bag. I think they're pretty funny. But my friends think they're lame. Should I tell my dad to stop?

A That's totally up to you. If you like the drawings and aren't bothered by what your friends say, let your dad keep drawing the cartoons. But if you don't want to deal with your friends' comments, ask your dad to draw on a notecard instead. He can tuck the card inside your lunch bag. Then you can still enjoy the pictures but share them only if you want to.

Q The lunch lines at my school are so long, there's hardly any time to eat! What can I do?

A Could you bring a bag lunch? It's a little extra work in the morning, but you won't have to wait in line to get your food. You could also keep a snack handy, like a granola bar—something you can eat quickly on your way back to class.

Talk to your parents about the long-line situation. Maybe a group of kids and parents could get together and talk to the school staff. If enough people say something, the school may change the way it does lunch.

Getting Organized

Q I can't find things in my desk, and sometimes I have a hard time shutting my locker door. How can I be better organized?

A Go through your stuff often. Recycle old worksheets, throw out the garbage, and bring home the things you don't need at school anymore. If you make a habit of doing this, it won't take long at all. Once you're down to the things you absolutely need, try using shelves, bins, pouches, magnetic clips, and hooks. There are all sorts of things made to organize lockers and desks. Do you know kids whose desks or lockers are always neat? Ask them for advice.

Q I'm always the last one to finish a worksheet or a test. And it takes me forever to finish my homework. How can I make my brain work faster?

A Everyone's brain works a little differently. But the more you worry about how slow you are, the slower you'll be! So stop worrying. You do your work carefully, and that's a good thing. Kids who race through their work often make mistakes.

Q I daydream a lot in school. What can I do to make myself pay attention?

A Daydreaming is a problem for a lot of people. But it can be a good thing too. It means you have an imagination! When you are in school, though, you need to focus. Are there any patterns to your daydreaming? Is it harder to pay attention right before lunch? Maybe you need to eat a better breakfast. Then your energy will last until it's time to eat. Is it harder to pay attention near the end of the day? Maybe you need fresh air or exercise at recess. Do you daydream more in some classes than in others? If you tune things out because a subject is hard for you, ask your teacher for help.

Try wearing a rubber band around your wrist. When you start to drift, "snap out of it" by lightly snapping the rubber band.

Dream

Love

Live

Tip Clip

As you go through the school day, set aside the things you'll need to take home. Then you'll have everything you need by the end of the day.

Q A couple kids on my bus were playing with a lighter. That's definitely against the rules. The bus driver didn't see. Should I tell? I don't want anyone to get mad at me.

A Sometimes you have to do the right thing whether or not anyone gets mad at you. If the kids on your bus are doing something dangerous, you should tell the driver. What if someone gets hurt? Wouldn't you feel bad if you didn't speak up? Once the bus driver knows what's going on, he or she can keep an eye on things.

Q Some kids are really rough on the playground. I'm afraid that I might get hurt. What can I do?

A Talk to the kids and ask them to tone it down. Or go play in another part of the playground, away from them. If that doesn't work, tell your playground monitor what's going on. Get some of your friends to go with you, so the monitor will see that the rough play is bothering other kids too. If the monitor doesn't do anything, talk to your teacher, principal, or parents.

Q I saw a boy in our class cheat on a test. I want to say something to the teacher, but what if he finds out I told on him?

A Go ahead and tell your teacher. It's the right thing to do. But wait for a time when you're alone and no one else can hear you. Or write your teacher a note or an e-mail. Describe exactly what you saw, and then let your teacher handle it. Most teachers won't let on who told.

Of course, the boy might guess it was you. If he gets mad, try to stay calm. Don't talk about it with anyone else—that will only make things worse. Whatever happens, remember that you didn't do anything wrong. He did.

Tip Clip

It's better to get a bad grade honestly than a good grade by cheating. If you're tempted to cheat because your parents are pressuring you to get good grades, talk to them about it.

Glossary

autistic—having a condition that causes a person to have trouble communicating and forming connections with others

bullying—being mean and hurtful to another person on purpose, again and again

clique—a group of friends who do not accept others into their group

compromise—to reach an agreement in which each side gives up part of its demands

distract—to draw attention away from something

extra—a person who plays a minor, usually nonspeaking part in a play or movie; also called a background actor

food allergy—a condition that makes a person very sick when he or she breathes in, touches, or eats a certain food

fund-raiser—an event meant to raise money for a cause or project

monitor—a person who watches over things and makes sure people follow the rules

pressure—a strong force or influence

prop—an object used by an actor or performer during a show; short for "property"

respect—to believe in the quality and worth of others and yourself

silent auction—an event at which people write down how much they are willing to pay for an item; the person who writes down the highest amount gets the item

tease—to make fun of someone

Read More

Espeland, Pamela, and Elizabeth Verdick. *See You Later, Procrastinator!: (Get It Done).* Laugh & Learn. Minneapolis: Free Spirit Pub., 2008.

Kilpatrick, Haley, with Whitney Joiner. *The Drama Years: Real Girls Talk About Surviving Middle School—Bullies, Brands, Body Image, and More.* New York: Free Press, 2012.

Montalbano, Julie Williams. *Smart Girl's Guide, Middle School: Everything You Need to Know About Juggling More Homework, More Teachers, and More Friends!* A Smart Girl's Guide. Middleton, Wisc.: American Girl, 2014.

Internet Sites

FactHound offers a safe, fun way to find Internet sites related to this book. All of the sites on FactHound have been researched by our staff.

Here's all you do:

Visit *www.facthound.com*

Type in this code: 9781491418611

Index

For my fourth-grade teacher, Miss Stenzel—NL

For the Little Harbor School community who created Lydia's memorial garden—PS

Snap Books are published by Capstone Press, 1710 Roe Crest Drive, North Mankato, Minnesota 56003 www.capstonepub.com

Library of Congress Cataloging-in-Publication Data
Cataloging-in-publication information is on file with the Library of Congress.

ISBN 978-1-4914-1861-1 (library binding)
ISBN 978-1-4914-1866-6 (eBook PDF)

Editorial Credits
Jill Kalz, editor; Juliette Peters, designer; Svetlana Zhurkin, media researcher; Charmaine Whitman, production specialist

Photo Credits
Getty Images: Jupiterimages, 9; iStockphotos: Christopher Futcher, cover, GlobalStock, 10, RichLegg, 26; Shutterstock: AntonioDiaz, 6, Elena Vasilchenko, 4, Jill Chen, 25, Kamira, 20—21, Lisa F. Young, 15, lzf, 16, Monkey Business Images, 12, 23, racorn, 19, Tyler Olson, 29, ZouZou, 11

Look for all the books in the series:

About the Consultant

John E. Desrochers, PhD, is a licensed psychologist and certified school psychologist who has worked for more than 30 years with children and families in schools, clinics, and private practice. He earned his doctorate in educational psychology at Columbia University and also holds graduate degrees in remedial reading, behavior analysis, and marriage and family therapy. John has numerous professional publications and was recognized with a School Psychologist of the Year Award by the National Association of School Psychologists.

About the Authors

Nancy Loewen has published many books for kids. She's a two-time Minnesota Book Award finalist (*Four to the Pole* and *The LAST Day of Kindergarten*) and the recipient of a Distinguished Achievement Award from the Association of Educational Publishers (Writer's Toolbox series). She holds an MFA from Hamline University in St. Paul. Nancy has two children and lives near Minneapolis. To learn more, visit *www.nancyloewen.com*.

Paula Skelley is a blogger who writes about life, loss, and pediatric cancer awareness. She holds a BS in English and sociology and an MA in English (creative writing concentration) from Minnesota State University, Mankato. She is a mother of two and lives in the New Hampshire Seacoast Region.

Nancy and Paula met years ago as English majors at MSU, Mankato, and they have been friends ever since. This is their first project together.

Printed in Canada.
092014 008478FRS15